North Korean Aviation

An Eyewitness Account

GERRY MANNING

Front cover image: Seconds from touchdown, Noth Korean Air Force MiG-21bis 42 (red) at Wonsan is flown by one of the nation's female pilots.

Back cover image: Air Koryo Ilyushin IL-62 P-885 lands at Wonsan following its display at the airshow.

Title page image: The tails of three types of airliner, all of which are now very rare. The Air Koryo Il-62, Tu-134 and Il-18 sit on the ramp at Wonsan.

Contents page image: Antonov An-24 P-537 returns to the ramp following a pleasure flight for the Western visitors.

Published by Key Books
An imprint of Key Publishing Ltd
PO Box 100
Stamford
Lincs PE19 1XQ

www.keypublishing.com

The right of Gerry Manning to be identified as the author of this book has been asserted in accordance with the Copyright, Designs and Patents Act 1988 Sections 77 and 78.

Copyright © Gerry Manning, 2021

ISBN 978 1 802820 37 9

Typeset by SJmagic DESIGN SERVICES, India.

Contents

Introduction

Most people have a bucket list of things they want to do or places they would like to visit. For this writer, North Korea was very high on my list. Why you may ask? The answer is because it is the only country in the world that is 'closed'. Not in the sense that you cannot go there and hopefully return from, they do have limited tourism, but because the resident population are cut off from news of the rest of the world. Even in the old USSR and East Germany residents were aware of what went on outside their borders even if they could not join in. However, the people in North Korea cannot access the World Wide Web and, if you are lucky enough to have one, the mobile telephones are local service only. The television and radio stations are state controlled and only broadcast approved stories of how well the nation is doing, and newspapers fall into the same trap. A copy of the English-language edition of the *Pyongyang Times* contained nothing but good news about North Korea but had a piece entitled 'South Korea, a Living Hell'. The population are taught from infants' school that they owe everything to the leaders and the party, and, since there is no evidence to contradict, this they will firmly believe they are living in a workers' paradise.

So how did Korea become like this and why? From 1910 to 1945, the whole of the Korean peninsula was a colony of Japan and under a very strict and brutal rule. The end of World War Two saw it divided along the line of the 38th parallel, the north under the control of the USSR and the south under the US. September 1948 saw the founding of the Democratic People's Republic of Korea (DPRK) under the leadership of Kim Il-sung, known forever as the Great Leader. At that time, most of the country's industry and natural resources were in the north and had been run by the Japanese, whilst in the south, it was mainly an agrarian society – how things have changed over the years! The north's economy is in freefall while the south, now known as the Republic of Korea, is one of the leading economies in the world.

Becoming a Tourist

In 2016, it was announced that North Korea would hold its first ever airshow. Aviation tour companies were invited to run trips to this event. For aircraft enthusiasts, this was a not to be missed opportunity and Ian Allan Aviation Tours, in conjunction with UK-based North Korean experts Juche Travel Services, arranged to take a group to the show and for them to stay for a week to see some of the sites of the nation. Since there are no direct flights from the UK to North Korea, the plan was to have a short stopover in Beijing, China, and to fly to Pyongyang, the North Korean capital, on Air Koryo, the only airline in the country.

Chapter 1
The Adventure Starts

The early morning of Wednesday 21 September 2016 saw a mixed group of photographers, spotters and general aircraft enthusiasts checking in at London Heathrow's Terminal 3 for Finnair flight number AY832 to Helsinki, where we would take AY051 on to Beijing. Airbus A321 OH-LZH operated the first leg, and brand-new Airbus A350 OH-LWE delivered our group to the Chinese capital at 6.47am the following day. A visa was not needed as we were going to be in China under 72 hours. Since it was too early to go to the hotel, a coach took us to the Chinese Aviation Museum at Datang Shan, which houses one of the finest collections in the world. It is a huge site and some hours were spent with the many varied aircraft out in the open, in hangars and in a man-made tunnel carved out of a hillside.

Then it was off to the hotel to freshen up and have a meeting with the representatives from the tour company, who had arranged all the local North Korea plans. They were able to give a briefing on what to expect and the dos and don'ts. North Korea is not like most other nations and so the rules included:

1. Only take pictures once permission has been given.
2. Treat the social and political system with sensitivity and respect.
3. Do not import any works that criticise the nation, its leaders or political system.
4. Do not import films or DVDs showing other nations.
5. Do not bring in any pornographic material in any form.
6. Expect to be escorted at all times, when outside, by guides.
7. Do not import any religious materials, Bibles or similar publications.

Once the briefing was over, it was time for dinner and, since we had been up for many hours, an early night.

Into the Belly of the Beast

The next morning we found ourselves in Area E of Beijing Airport, where the check-in for Air Koryo was located. An excited crowd of aviation enthusiast were gathered. The flight number was JS152, departing at 12 noon, and seat selection was not available – you got what they gave you. The aircraft for the flight was waiting for us at Gate 9; it was a Tupolev Tu-204, registration P-633. We pushed back at 12.15pm, but air traffic control was very slow at Beijing and so we were in a queue for over 30 minutes before we became airborne. The interior seating was three seats either side of the aisle in an all-economy configuration, making a total of 210 seats. Air Koryo is rated as the only one-star airline in the world and reported to be the worst on earth. Is this justified? The answer is a firm no. The legroom was fine, and we were served a snack if we wanted one. There was no seat-back screen for films but small overhead ones at points along the cabin showed a concert by a well-known, all-women army band but without any sound. The short, 84-minute, flight was no better or worse than many airlines in the West.

We had, at last, arrived in North Korea and soon learned that the locals preferred us to use the term DPRK. Pyongyang Airport was quiet, and the travel company organisers were splitting the visitors

普通舱
Economy Class

고려항공
AIR KORYO

The adventure starts with check-in at Beijing for our flight to the Hermit Kingdom.

into the long- and the short-tour groups. I was in the former and was handed a boarding pass, with no name or seat number, for a flight to Kalma International Airport at Wonsan, where the airshow was to take place over the following two days.

It was there that we would officially enter the country, as Pyongyang was only a transit stop. I was delighted to find the aircraft for the long-tour group was an Ilyushin IL-62, P-885, operating flight number JS6201. Since I was one of the first on board I took seat 1B, one of 33 first-class seats; there were 136 economy seats further back. The IL-62 is now a very rare aircraft with just a handful still in the air, either as freighters or government VIP equipped. The interior of our ride was almost unchanged since the 1960s with no overhead bins but, instead, open shelves, which would have been for hats and coats. We departed at local time 15.30pm; local time was 30 minutes ahead of Beijing time. The flight time to Wonsan was just 20 minutes and so no in-flight service was provided or expected.

We then began the process of legal entry into the country. We had been given three forms; the first went to Quarantine and was taken without a comment. The next point of call was Immigration and once again the form was taken without any fuss. I was beckoned to Customs and asked for my passport, visa, customs form and mobile phone. The official then asked where my luggage was, and when I said that it had not yet arrived I was instructed to go back and wait for it. Our cases had not been sorted at Pyongyang and had been put on either the IL-62 I had flown on or the Tupolev Tu-154 the short-stay tourists had arrived on. It was over 30 minutes later that my case appeared on the luggage carousel. During that time, I had often looked back at the customs official, as he had my passport and phone, and we would both shrug our shoulders with a smile in the globally understood expression of 'still waiting'. By the time I returned with my case we were almost friends, and, despite him being very thorough, I was soon landside. It took some time for all of our particular group, which consisted of 14 people from the UK, Ireland and Japan, to get through the airport and meet our three guides.

The Tupolev Tu-204 was first flown from Ulyanovsk in January 1989. Its role was to replace the fleet of Tu-154s operated by the USSR's national flag carrier Aeroflot and those of other operators of the type in countries friendly to the USSR. Power came from a pair of Perm PS-90A turbofans with an output of 35,580lb st. By the time its test flying was finished, the political arena in the USSR had changed, and the newly independent republics that used to make up the USSR and Eastern-bloc nations were able to buy or lease Western-built designs. This resulted in low Tu-204 sales with few in passenger services and the rest undertaking cargo operations. Pictured at Pyongyang airport in September 2016, having operated Air Koryo flight number JS152 from Beijing, is Tu-204-100V P-633 c/n 1450741964048.

We had been told that the hotels we were staying in at Wonsan would be allocated upon arrival. Upon asking the guides about this, we were informed we were to stay at the Kiddie Camp, to which the response was: 'Sorry I thought you said the Kiddie Camp'. 'That is correct', they replied. This turned out to be the Songdowon International Children's Camp. Fortunately, the camp did not consist of tented accommodation but was a large sports complex where local and invited international children could practise all sorts of sports at the excellent facilities. A fleet of small buses ferried the groups there. The living area had seven floors, and at the end of the corridor, by the lift, was a table with two ladies keeping an eye on the activities of the floor. When I reached my solo-occupancy sixth-floor room, I found I had a choice of five single pink beds, from which I can only assume it was usually a girls' room. All the children who would normally be resident had been moved out.

It was then downstairs for what was to be a common activity – paying our respects to past leaders. All 14 of us were asked to line up and march forward to a statue of Kim Il-sung (Great Leader) and his son Kim Jong-il (Dear Leader), portraying them with six happy, smiling children. Our Tour Manager then walked ahead to lay flowers as the rest of us were asked to bow. With our three guides was a video man who filmed our activities for the week to come, and a copy could be purchased at the end of the trip. It was then time for dinner and a buffet line for the food. We had a tray with indented areas to hold the food. The selection included luke-warm rice, fish and a type of spring roll, as well as green tea. It was then time to have a beer and chat with the others or to go to bed.

Above: A Kiddie Camp bedroom. Despite being furnished with five single pink beds, it was used for solo occupancy.

Opposite: Floor view of the Kiddie Camp interior – note the two people on floor two keeping an eye on what happens on that level.

Below: A statue of the Great Leader and Dear Leader with happy children at the camp.

Chapter 2
The Airshow

After a good night's sleep in one of the five pink beds, my alarm clock woke me at 6.00am, in time for a shower. It took some time to run the water before it could be considered hot enough, perhaps because I was on the sixth floor. Breakfast was a buffet and included fish, rice, toast, crisps, boiled eggs and green tea. It was also a chance to get some water for the day as the sun was shining. I handed in a 5€ note and got four bottles and US$4 change.

The 7.20am departure saw a fleet of small buses take us to the town square in Wonsan. There we found statues of both the Great Leader and Dear Leader and lots of North Korean reporters and photographers to cover the moment when a large bouquet of flowers was placed in front of the statues and we were all asked to bow. It was then back on the buses to go to the airport for the show. We arrived via the terminal. Kalma International Airport is very new and is a fine building, but it does not have any regular services at the moment. There was a standard airport security check to get airside and, once out, there were five Air Koryo airliners to be photographed in the morning sunshine. They were Tupolevs Tu-134 and Tu-154, Ilyushins IL-18 and IL-62, and an Antonov An-24.

It was soon time to walk across the runway to the other side of the airfield for the 10.00am opening of the show. The authorities had invited up to 250 Western visitors to attend the event and approximately 150 had taken them up on their invitation. This is hardly a crowd for such an event

The first morning's flowers being presented to the statue of the Great Leader at Wonsan – note the number of local media.

The airshow commentators – note both have the little red badge.

so some 15,000 local workers arrived to sit on the grass and watch. One group sported blue baseball caps while another had white ones and a third, yellow. A man with an armband was making notes and seemed to be in charge of them. The locals were enjoying themselves, as they were having a day off work and were able to sit in the sun and watch an airshow, the first in the country.

To open the event, there were speeches of welcome in Korean and English, with the English commentary being given by a man and the Korean by a woman in a hanbok, a traditional Korean dress. Both wore, as do most of the population, a small red badge with pictures of both the Great Leader and Dear Leader. It should be noted that only these two have pictures all over the nation; the current leader Kim Jong-un has no statues or pictures, yet.

The airshow crowd; each different hat colour represents a different work place.

The first event of the airshow was a solo display by a McDonnell Douglas (formally Hughes) MD500, a US-built light observation and attack helicopter. This is not what you would expect to see in North Korea with all the sanctions and embargoes on trade between the two nations. Their acquisition dates back to the 1980s when, via a West German dealer, North Korea obtained over 80 airframes. However, as soon as it was discovered who the end user was, trade was halted. The display was very good at showing off the machine to the delight of the crowd, who had never seen such antics in a helicopter.

Next was the take-off and display of the Ilyushin IL-18. Few airshows will feature a four-engine, 100-seat airliner in their line-up, and it was most welcome to see this classic turboprop make a series of flypasts. Whilst it was still in the air, the next item was seen taxiing to the runway. This was one of the aircraft on display that few people ever expected to see – the MiG-29 in the full markings of the Korean People's Army Air Force (KPAAF). Until we landed at Wonsan, nobody knew for certain what we were going to see. We had visions of airliners with some military aircraft simply flying past at altitude from another base. However, the sight of a number of fast jets in sheds at the side of the runway made everyone's spirits rise. We then knew that the extremely rare aircraft were here and going to be displayed and photographed in the sunshine.

The MiG-29 put on a great show and landed streaming a drag chute to slow it down. It was now becoming apparent that we were getting a civil airliner then a military aircraft. Following the MiG-29 was a Tupolev Tu-134 airliner, then a Sukhoi Su-25 ground-attack aircraft followed by a Tu-154. Helicopters came back in the form of four MD500s, which put on a stunning display that would have had them banned from any airshow in the West, as they flew at, and at times over, the crowd; it was a great sight to behold.

Soon it was 12 noon and a two-hour break for lunch. We walked back across the runway to the terminal for a fine buffet lunch, which mainly consisted of salad items. It was also time to examine the contents of a carrier bag we had each been given. One item was a programme of events for the two-day show and the other was quite a surprise – it was a towel marked 'Wonsan Air Festival'. When we asked about this, we were told that we might be sitting on the grass and it could be wet. It was a very thoughtful gesture, and never have I seen such an item given out elsewhere. The programme had listed the two-hour morning as 'Opening ceremony, aviation skill display and beer drinking'. As well as being an airshow, the event was also a beer festival. Not being a drinker myself, I cannot comment on the quality of the beer. However, I was told by those who imbibed that it was good.

The nation's flag arrives by parachute.

By 2.00pm, the sun had moved around and our request to stay over on the terminal side of the airfield, as the sun would be behind us, was granted, and we were able to stand close to the taxiway. The first two aircraft of the afternoon session were a pair of sanction busters: a New Zealand-built Pacific Aerospace P-750 XSTOL and an Italian-designed Alpi Pioneer 400. Neither displayed any identification so how they arrived in North Korea is not confirmed. However, it was alleged that the P-750 had been delivered via China. During the afternoon, we were treated to an Ilyushin IL-62, an Antonov An-24, a Mi-17 helicopter, an Ilyushin IL-76, a trio of Sukhoi Su-25s and, finally, a pair of MiG-21s. The latter two were piloted by two young women.

The last of the flying finished at 4.00pm, giving us time to return to the other side of the airfield to see what was on sale at the various stalls that had been set up. There were model aircraft kits and other items, and, of course, there was beer if you wanted some. Many of the locals were drinking and I noticed some of the Western visitors would raise their glass with a smile, which would be returned by the locals in an international gesture of friendship when there is a language barrier.

Departure was at 4.30pm for an early dinner. It was then on to the Songdowon Youth Open Air Theatre for a song and dance performance by Kangwon Provincial Art Troupe. The show was very entertaining and of a high standard, but the seats were the most uncomfortable I have ever sat on. The venue was full, with several thousand people present. Soon it was back to the Kiddie Camp to put the camera battery on charge and change the memory card; I had taken over 800 shots in one day. So ended the first full day in North Korea.

Both MiG-21s were flown by female pilots, who were all but mobbed as local celebrities.

The next day, a Sunday, had a 7.00am departure. When our bus was still over a mile away from the airport, we passed several thousand people walking in groups of over 100 at a time, all on their way to the show to make up the crowd of spectators. Once through security, an airport bus took us to the Ilyushin IL-76 parked at one end of the airfield so that we could take static shots of it. The staff were very obliging and even moved traffic cones and a car that were in the shot.

The second day of the show opened with model aircraft and parachutists, one trailing the nation's flag, a second the flag of the Worker's Party of Korea, the founding and ruling political party of North Korea. A third was shooting flares from an attachment on his ankle. The parachutists were all members of the Pyongyang Air Club and jumped from an air force Mi-8 helicopter. A few lucky Western visitors

had also signed up to jump either free fall, if you had a certificate to say you had done so previously, or in a tandem jump strapped to an experienced local. Those who did would be able to boast about 'the day they parachuted into North Korea' for years to come!

We had the opportunity to take static shots of the MiG-21, MiG-29, Su-25 and MD500. During the shoot, the air crew arrived. The two MiG-21 pilots were young women and were all but mobbed by the local press, as they were local celebrities. The male pilots of the other fast jets could only look on, as few people bothered to take their picture.

There was no display flying on the second day, but, both before and after lunch, the airliners and helicopters were busy doing pleasure flights. New additions to the types on display were several Antonov An-2s or Yunshuji Y-5s, the Chinese licence-built version, as the KPAAF operate both. The show ended with more speeches and we were bussed to Haean Square in the centre of Wonsan for what we had been told was a dance display. It was not what we expected. There was no small stage with Korean folk dancing in national costumes but the sight of some five to six thousand couples ballroom dancing to music from loud speakers while lit by floodlight. All the men wore the same outfit of black trousers, white shirt and red tie, and all had the small badge with the images of both the Great and Dear Leaders. The women all wore the same style of dress but in many different colours and patterns and, again, the little red badges. As our groups departed the whole crowd stopped to give us a round of applause. It can only be described as surreal! A farewell dinner with yet more speeches followed at a very elaborate building with chandeliers and marble columns. After this it was back to the Kiddie Camp for our last night there.

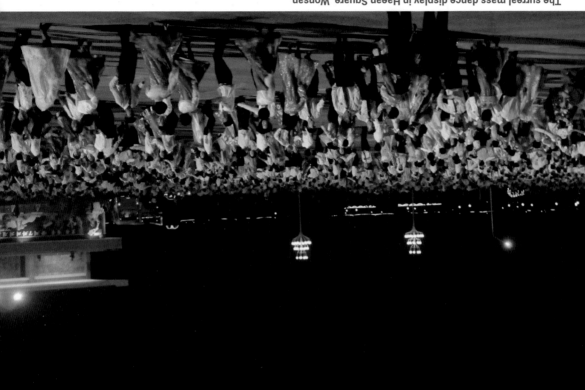

The surreal mass dance display in Haean Square, Wonsan.

Above, below and opposite: Ilyushin IL-62M P-885 c/n 3933913 shows off its graceful lines. Again, Air Koryo is one of the few operators still flying the type. The IL-62 first flew in January 1961, and it was a long-range airliner with four rear-mounted Soloviev D-30K turbofans with an output of 25,350lb st. The 'M' variant had extra fuel tanks in the vertical fin. This aircraft had 33 first class and 136 economy seats.

Above, below and opposite: The Mikoyan-Gurevich MiG-21 (NATO reporting name *Fishbed*) is one of the most famous of all the fighters from that design bureau. It serves, or has served, with no fewer than 49 air arms, including perhaps the most secret of them all, the Korean People's Army Air Force (KPAAF). MiG-21bis 53 and its companion, 42, were on show.

Above: The badge on MiG-21bis 42.

Below and opposite: The US-built McDonnell Douglas (formally Hughes) MD500 light observation and attack helicopter is not one that you would expect to see in KPAAF service because of embargoes on trade between the two nations. To the delight of the crowd, the helicopter performed manoeuvres that had never been seen before. The MD500 was famous for its aerobatic ability.

Above, below and opposite: With a first flight dating back to July 1957, the Ilyushin IL-18 was a long-range airliner powered by four IVP AI-20M turboprops. As with the IL-62, Air Koryo are amongst the last to still operate the type. IL-18D P-835 c/n 188011205 was equipped with 100 economy seats and on the first day did a display, while on the second it operated a pleasure flight.

Above, below and opposite: The most potent of all the fighters in the KPAAF is the MiG-29 (NATO reporting name *Fulcrum*). Two examples, 555 and 550, were on show, and at the end of their display, 555 streamed a drag-chute to slow it down on the runway. The KPAAF have operated the type since 1988 and are one of nearly 30 air arms to do so.

Above, left and opposite:
The USSR in World War Two had one of the first dedicated ground-attack aircraft in the form of the Ilyushin IL-2 Shturmovik, and its jet successor is the Sukhoi Su-25 (NATO reporting name *Frogfoot*). The Su-25 has no fewer than ten underwing hard points for the carriage of various weapons and features wing tip speed brakes.

Above, below and opposite: Following the solo display by the MD500, a four-ship team performed an excellent routine to show how manoeuvrable the type could be.

Above and below: New Zealand-designed and built, the Pacific Aerospace P-750 XSTOL is a utility aircraft powered by a single 750shp Pratt & Whitney Canada PT-6 turboprop. As well as its single pilot, it can carry nine passengers or up to 17 parachutists. How this new design arrived in North Korea with all the sanctions that are in place is not clear. However, it is believed to be one that was sold to a company in China and then illegally exported to North Korea. The aircraft did not display any identification.

Above and below: Another sanctions-busting type was an unmarked Alpi Pioneer 400. It is an Italian-designed, four-seat, ultra-light sport aircraft. It is sold either as a kit for home construction or as a complete airframe ready to fly. Power comes from a single Rotax 912S piston engine with an output of 98hp. How it arrived in North Korea is unknown.

Above, below and opposite: In the West, the first turboprops for regional services included the Avro 748, Fokker F27 and the Handley Page Dart Herald. In this class, the USSR produced the Antonov An-24, a twin-engine airliner powered by a pair of IVP AI-24A turboprops. It can still be found in limited service in parts of the world. Air Koryo AN-24B P-537 c/n 67302408 is configured with 50 economy seats.

Opposite, above and right: The USSR was renowned for their large helicopters; many are today leased by the United Nations for operations providing aid to victims of natural disasters. The main design bureau for helicopters was led by Dr Mikhail Mil, and the Mil designation was used on all their types. The Mi-17 was a modified Mi-8 (the NATO reporting name for both was *Hip*) with systems from the Mi-14 and the tail rotor now on the starboard side. Two TV-3-117MT turboshafts powered the type. Mi-17 847 of the KPAAF is configured as a VIP aircraft and, as can be seen, it has a very unusual interior layout.

Above, below, opposite and overleaf pages: One of the most widely used heavy freighters operating in both civil and military operations is the Ilyushin IL-76. Powered by four 26,445lb st Aviadvigatel D-30KP turbofans, it first flew in March 1971. Despite being a freighter, Air Koryo IL-76TD P-913 c/n 1003404126 was offering pleasure flights for those who wanted to fly in types that they would normally not be able to travel on.

Above, below and opposite: In the afternoon of the first day, a trio of Sukhoi Su-25Ks – 28, 45 and 57 – performed a number of flypasts in a loose formation.

Above, below and opposite: One of the most widely used helicopters built in the USSR was the Mil Mi-8 (NATO reporting name *Hip*). It had many roles including transport, attack and electronic warfare, and was even used as a command post. Over 50 air arms use, or have used, the type. Mi-8s 303 and 312 were used at the show for parachute jumping and pleasure flights.

Above, below and opposite: Despite being a slow piston-engined biplane, the Antonov An-2 (NATO reporting name *Colt*) has many uses owing to its ability to fly very slowly and land and take-off from almost any location. The design has been built in the USSR, but the bulk of the production was from a plant in Poland. It has also been manufactured in China as the Yunshuji Y-5. The aircraft used by the KPAAF are believed to be a mix from both the Chinese and Polish production lines. An-2T 952 c/n 1G129-52 was operating pleasure flights with 621. As it was not possible to confirm the variant, that aircraft could have been either a Y-5 or an An-2.

Above, below and opposite: First flown in July 1963, the Tupolev Tu-134 was a short-haul airliner powered by a pair of rear-mounted Soloviev D-30 turbofans with an output of 14,990lb st. Air Koryo Tu-134B-3 P-813 c/n 66215 both displayed and offered pleasure flights on different days at the show. The B-3 variant had upgraded engines, and the seating configuration for this aircraft is 76 all-economy seats. Very few Tu-134s remain in airline service, and those that do tend to be in use as corporate jets.

Above, below and opposite: The role of the Tupolev Tu-154 was that of a medium-range airliner, and it was powered by a trio of rear-mounted Kuznetsov NK-8 turbofans. It was the most widely used airliner in the USSR during the 1980s and 1990s. Air Koryo Tu-154B P-522 c/n 76A143, like all the fleet at the show, both displayed and offered pleasure flights. As with the Tu-134, few are to be found in commercial service today.

Chapter 3

North Korea on the Ground

Monday morning saw many of the Western visitors going home, but our group of 14 were staying on as tourists for a few more days. It seemed to me that if you had gone to all the trouble to come to the country, it was worth staying to see some more of it that just the airshow. Following the usual breakfast, we departed at 7.00am for the airport. Sights seen during the journey included workers doing group morning exercises in front of their factories, a mother taking two children to school on her bicycle, a 12-piece band playing in the street and lots of people on bikes but few cars. One woman had a large bundle on her head, a traditional way to carry such loads.

When we reached Kalma Airport there was not a single vehicle in the car park. Security was quick, as we only had hand baggage, the cases having stayed on the bus to be driven to the hotel in Pyongyang. On the departures board were just three flights, two to the capital. One of them had already departed and the second was due out at 8.40am, oddly both had the same flight number of JS6302. Our flight to Samjiyon, at 8.30am, was number JS6732. Out on the ramp was Antonov An-24B P-537. The airliner was powered by a pair of IV AI-24 turboprops and had 50 all-economy seats in a two either side of the aisle layout. Again, there were no overhead bins just the old open hat and coat shelf that the flight crew of three had left their hats on. We could sit anywhere as the flight was not full.

Flying over the northern part of North Korea, we took note of the often bleak landscape and inhospitable terrain. The flight lasted 54 minutes and there were no other aircraft at Samjiyon when

A school run North Korean style.

we arrived. A walk through the single-storey terminal led us to another bus (almost all were the same type) for a trip through some miles of forest and open hillsides, all the time climbing in altitude to over 7,000ft (2,133.6m). The engine of the bus did have to struggle because of the thin air. The reason for this journey was a visit to Mount Paektu. It is a volcanic peak on the border with China and has been important in both the culture and mythology of the Korean nation. It was in this area that the Great Leader Kim Il-sung organised resistance to the Japanese forces occupying the country. There is also a story that his son, Dear Leader Kim Jong-il, was born there, although it is much more likely that he was, in fact, born in the USSR.

We took a funicular railway up to the 9,000ft (2,743m) peak, where the view was spectacular. Below us was Heaven Lake, a crater lake, and across in the distance a house could be seen on a high point. This dwelling was actually in China, as we were right on the border. Our next stop was the Samji Grand Monument, where we were shown a large 49ft 2in (15m) statue of the Great Leader, depicting him as a young man during the period when he fought the Japanese. There were also large sculptures showing scenes commemorating the Battle of Pochonbo against the occupying Japanese. They show the guerrilla army, their supporters and camp followers. The scale of these are very impressive and only with a person in the picture can their size truly be appreciated.

It was then back to Samjiyon Airport and our An-24 for the 74-minute flight to Pyongyang as JS6733. Since we were a domestic arrival and the luggage had gone on ahead, it was a swift departure from the airport and a 40-minute bus ride to the smart-looking Hotel Koryo, our home for the next four nights. Following dinner, I popped into the hotel shop for some snacks. The system was straight out of the old USSR. You pick your items off the shelf and take them to a counter, and the person there writes out a chit. You then take this to the cashier to pay, Euros or US dollars, and the cashier then stamps your chit. You take it back to the original counter were it is checked, and then you can have the items you have purchased. I suppose it does keep more people in work.

Monday morning 7.00am band practice at Wonsan.

Workers' morning exercise at Wonsan.

The northern North Korean landscape seen from the air.

The shadow of the Antonov An-24 as it approaches to land at Samjiyon.

Samjiyon Airport terminal.

Above: The landscape en route to Mount Paektu.

Left: The funicular railway up to Mount Paektu.

Heaven Lake, a crater lake 9,000ft (2,743.2m) above sea level on Mount Paektu. The land in the far distance is the border with China.

This building, pictured from Mount Paektu, is in China.

This 49ft 2in (15m) tall statue of the Great Leader, as young man, is at Samji Grand Monument.

A local crowd bows to the statue of the Great Leader at Samji Grand Monument.

One of the series of statues at Samji Grand Monument. The person in front gives an idea of the scale of the figures.

A City to Explore

Breakfast was a buffet with lots of unknown local items, but one chef was cooking eggs while another was making toast, so I had a couple of fried eggs on toast to set me up for the morning. We departed at 8.00am on an overcast, but not cold, day; it had been raining during the night. The first visit was to a series of ornamental fountains followed by the Mansudae Grand Monument. Here, historical scenes, where amazing details can be seen on the many figures displayed, flank giant statues of both the Great Leader and Dear Leader, at the bases of which people lay flowers. The next port of call was a library in a beautiful building. In one room, students were learning the thoughts of the Great Leader, while in another, they were on North Korea's own internet. One book caught our attention; it was by the current leader, Kim Jong-un, and was entitled *On bringing about a revolutionary turn in land administration in line with the demands for building a thriving socialist country.*

On then to the vast Kim Il-sung Square, a space that can hold tens of thousands of people. This led us to the foreign book shop were many other titles by the current leader were on sale, including *Let us usher in a great golden age of construction by thoroughly applying the party's Juche-oriented idea on architecture.* Outside the book shop was a crossroads, and we could see one of the famous traffic ladies in action. They are selected for their beauty and operate almost like a drill display when they move; I have seen it reported that they are retired at the age of 26.

The Juche Tower was next with a cost of 5€ to go up to the top, 560ft (170m) above the street level, to see the views of the city. Sadly, there was still a lot of haze so not a great view. The tower opened in 1982 and was designed by the Dear Leader himself. The term 'Juche' crops up a lot in North Korea. It is, at its most simple meaning, their idea of socialism to be one of self-reliance. Close to the tower was the Worker's Party structure, which could only be described as having a very austere style of architecture.

The afternoon was largely spent at the Victorious Fatherland Liberation War Museum, which commemorated the war known in the West as the Korean War. The museum's English-speaking guide

Mansudae Grand Monument, Pyongyang.

Right: **The statue of the Great Leader in Pyongyang. The people laying flowers give it some scale.**

Below: **Kim Il-sung Square in Pyongyang.**

Above left and above right: The famous Pyongyang traffic police are picked for their looks and retired at 26.

told us that the war had been started by American aggression and that North Korea had won. In reality, the war has not actually ended. An armistice was signed in July 1953, and the Demilitarized Zone (DMZ) was created, but no peace treaty was ever signed, and so the two Korean nations are technically still at war with each other.

We then headed to a Metro station for a ride on the underground train; the stations are very smart and the trains spotless and frequent. The station we came out at was the site of the Arch of Triumph, based upon the one in Paris but, of course, larger. That evening at dinner a video was playing in the restaurant showing the Moranbong Band, an all-female music group whose original members were personally selected by current leader Kim Jong-un. The members are all either instrumentalist or singers, and they hold army ranks. The reason they drew our attention was because they had on stage with them a MiG-19 fighter jet. There are many videos of them on YouTube. Back in in my hotel room, I was able to catch up on some of the happenings in the world by watching on TV the English-language version of the Russian RT news station; this would not be available to most of the local population in their own homes.

Right: A bill board that says that following a Worker's Party Conference, it had been decided that more production was required, so all the workers had 'volunteered' to work 200 extra days.

Below: A Pyongyang Metro station.

Metro workers wait for the next train.

In Pyongyang is the Victorious Fatherland Liberation War Museum. It commemorates what is known in the West as the Korean War. A number of aircraft from both sides are on show, the US ones being wrecks that had been shot down. Not flying until 1946, the Lavochkin La-9 (NATO reporting name *Fritz*) was too late for World War Two. It was an escort fighter and an all-metal development of the earlier La-5 and La-7. Power was from a single 1,850hp ASh-82FM piston engine. The preserved example is number 102.

Used during World War Two, the Yakovlev Yak-9P (NATO reporting name *Frank*) was an all-metal development of the Yak-3 and looked very similar. It was powered by a single VK-107A 1,700hp piston engine. Over 16,000 were built and the aircraft on show carries the number 12.

The Yakovlev Yak-18 (NATO reporting name *Max*) was a widely used primary training aircraft. Powered by a single 180hp piston engine, it first flew in 1946. The original model had a tail wheel undercarriage and a very distinctive helmet cowling. The one on show displays the serial number 03.

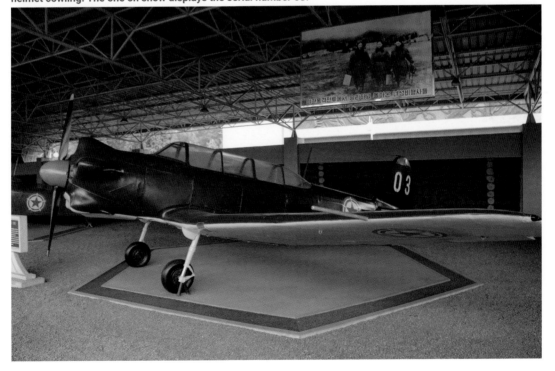

Above and below: Two examples of the MiG-15bis (NATO reporting name *Fagot*) single-seat fighter are on display – they are numbered 1032 and 009. The design was first flown in 1947 and was used extensively during the Korean War. It has been built in three countries and used by the air forces of many Soviet-friendly countries.

A line-up of the preserved North Korean exhibits of the war.

There were a number of American aircraft that were shot down on show. Since they were crashes, no attempt has been made to restore then, and they are as found. Two examples of the Douglas AD-5N Skyraider are present. The role of the aircraft was ground-attack and it could carry bombs, napalm, mines, rockets and other weapons from the many hard points under the wings, as can been seen.

The Skyraider was powered by a single 2,700hp Wright R-3350 air-cooled radial piston engine. Rear Admiral John W Hoskins of the US Navy described it as 'the best and most effective close support airplane in the world'. This example shows the barrels of the 20mm cannons.

With a World War Two Pacific campaign heritage, the Vought F4U-4 Corsair was used during the Korean War in a ground-attack role by the US Navy and the US Marine Corps. Its production run was from a first flight in 1940 to the end of 1952, when the last model rolled off the production line.

Only the rear fuselage and wing are left on this Douglas B-26C Invader 44-35210. It was a twin-engine light bomber powered by 2,000hp Pratt & Whitney R-2800 radial pistons. It started life as the A-26 ('A' for 'Attack'). However, in 1948, the 'Attack' category was abolished and it became the B-26. During World War Two, the Martin Marauder was known as the B-26, but, by 1948, there were none left in service. The museum has a picture of the Martin aircraft purporting to show what the complete aircraft on show would look like.

Above: The main USAF fighter in the war was the North American F-86 Sabre. As can be seen, not a lot is left of F-86D 52-10031. The MiG-15, its main opponent, was in many flight regimes superior to the Sabre, but well-trained US pilots had a better kill ratio. The power plant for the Sabre was a General Electric J-47.

Right: This Grumman F9F-2 Panther is almost unrecognisable. It was a single-seat, straight-wing, carrier-based fighter armed with four 20mm cannons and powered by a single Pratt & Whitney turbojet.

This Hiller OH-23D (UH-12D) Raven 61-3094 is not from the Korean War but at least a decade later. Having crossed the border accidently, it was captured. In the background is a picture of the two US Army crew with their hands up. The role of the helicopter was observation or basic flying training.

Moored in the Pothong River, by the museum, is the US Navy ship USS *Pueblo* (AGER-2). It was operated as a spy ship and captured by the North Koreans in January 1968. Both sides dispute its location at the time it was seized. The US stated that it was in international waters whilst the North Koreans maintained that it was in their territorial waters. The crew were held for 11 months and badly treated before being released. The ship is still officially a US Navy vessel and currently in commission, but it is unlikely ever to be taken back to the USA and paid off.

Above: The story of the USS *Pueblo* is being told to a group of locals as they listen intently.

Right: The storyteller is believed to be one of the crew who captured the ship – note the long line of medal ribbons on his chest.

Out of the City

An early start at 6.00am came with a packed breakfast, consisting of two pieces of toast, a hard-boiled egg, an apple, a can of iced coffee and a bottle of water. We were off to Hyangsan to visit the International Friendship Exhibition. It is the location of all the gifts that visiting delegations and VIPs have presented to North Korea's three leaders over the years. The roads were not in the best of condition for the three-hour plus journey. Half the group was on the bus and the other half flew in the air force Mi-17 that had been at the airshow. Those who flew went back in the bus and the group that arrived by bus flew back. The original plan was for two helicopters to be used, but only one was available.

Left: In the rural setting of Hyangsan is the International Friendship Exhibition. This is the home of all the gifts that delegations have presented to the country's leaders over the years.

Below: Visitors arrive to view the exhibition at Hyangsan.

A line-up of Air Koryo airliners at Pyongyang's main airport. They include a Tu-154, a pair of Tu-204s, an IL-62 and a pair of Tu-134s.

The newest airliner type in the Air Koryo fleet is the Ukrainian-built Antonov An-148B P-671 c/n 0308. It is a twin-engine regional jet that first flew in December 2004. As yet, not many aircraft have been produced. It is seen here at Pyongyang.

Tupolev Tu-154B-2 P-561 c/n 83A573 of Air Koryo is pictured at Pyongyang. Compare and contrast the newer livery style of the example at the show. It is not known if this old colour scheme will be changed to the new one.

The building was new and set in landscaped grounds. The security checks to enter the building were far stricter than the ones we had had at the airport. No photography was allowed, which was a great pity as in the building there was an Ilyushin IL-14 that both the Great Leader and Dear Leader had used to travel the nation. Following our trip, we had lunch at a hotel before being taken to a Buddhist temple. As no state religion is allowed in North Korea, it was an unusual thing to see. It appears that the state accepts Buddhism, not as a religion but more as a philosophy.

It was then all aboard the Mi-17 for our trip back to Pyongyang. The interior was somewhat of a surprise for an air force helicopter. Its main seating was a normal household settee with antimacassars, and there was a small table with two swivel chairs and a couple of stools. The carpet was bright green with large flower patterns on it. Note that no mention has been made of seat belts – there were none. The sector took just 33 minutes and we flew at a height of 2,300ft (700m) with a flight number of JS5102. The arrival on the ramp at Pyongyang Airport gave us the opportunity to take some pictures of the airliners including one type we had not seen before, an Antonov An-148, the newest aircraft in the Air Koryo fleet. The arrivals board displayed only one domestic service, our Mi-17 in from Hyangsan, and just one international services, which was to and from Shenyang in China. Despite the airport being almost empty of passengers all the shops were open with a full complement of staff in place.

The arrivals board at North Korea's capital airport shows just one flight movement. This was our flight (JS5102) in the Mi-17 helicopter from Hyangsan. To say the airport is underused is an understatement. One day all that was listed was a flight to Shenyang in China and its return.

Dinner that evening was at a restaurant some distance from the hotel where the food was hot and a good selection was provided. On the way back we asked our guides to sing us a Korean song and they duly obliged. They asked for a Western one and one of our number began with 'Hey Jude' by the Beatles, and we all joined in on the chorus. Small things like a song can really bring people together.

Last Day Changes and Microlights

The plan for the last full day in the country was a trip to the Demilitarized Zone (DMZ) several hours to the south. It is the most heavily defended border in the world. Whilst having breakfast we were informed that we would not be going. When we asked for the reason, the answer was just 'problems'. (We later discovered that a North Korean soldier had managed to cross to the south and claim asylum.) We were asked to wait for an hour while alternative plans were made for the day. As it happened, the new plan turned out to be a very good one, although it was a pity to miss the DMZ visit.

Above, below and opposite: The Mirim Aviation Club in the Sadong district of Pyongyang opened in July 2016. It is used for microlight flying and is housed in a very smart building that is up to the standard of many fixed-base jet operators in the West. The aircraft flown is a three-seat machine known as the Kulbeol, or Honeybee, and is North Korea designed and built.

A visit to a local park saw lots of couples having their wedding pictures taken – note that both the bride and groom shown have the little red badge.

The Arch of Triumph, Pyongyang. It is modelled on the Arc de Triomphe in Paris but is, of course, 33ft (10m) higher.

Juche Tower, Pyongyang. It is 558ft (170m) high and opened in 1982.

A Pyongyang road at night.

The first visit of the day was to a new facility, a microlight airfield, and we were the first ever group from the West to visit, as it had only opened a few months earlier, in July. The building resembled the entrance to a four-star hotel, there was a balcony for viewing and a short hard runway. The microlight aircraft were a locally designed three-seater named Kulbeol, which translates as Honeybee. Pleasure flights were on offer, but they would only take one passenger at a time, and if the person was on the heavy side they were not permitted to fly.

Following this, it was on to a city park, and we could see the locals enjoying the open space. One thing that was popular was wedding photographs and a number of brides and grooms were getting their pictures taken. All the couples were seen to wear the little red badge with the two dead leaders on it. One local custom was for the groom to pour water from the stream in the park over the bride's hands.

A technology museum was the first stop in the afternoon, and everything from cars, trains, buses and rockets, was on show. We then arrived at the Children's Palace for the 5.00pm show. This was a large theatre seating at least 2,000 people and on the day we were there, it was full. We had very good seats so I had to wonder who got bumped off, as we had not planned to be there. The performance by the children was of a very high standard, both in music and dance, and the theatre was very well equipped with a moveable stage sliding into the wings and the orchestra pit rising at the end for applause for the musicians who had performed the music for the dance routines.

When we left it was time for some night photography. We had seen some of the buildings in the city lit up at night and asked if we could go out at night to take pictures. The request was granted the following day. One of the most impressive when lit up was the Arch of Triumph. It was then time for the final dinner followed by some more night photography.

Kim Il-sung Square at night.

Chapter 4

The Adventure Ends

We had an early, 6.00am, departure on the following day so a packed breakfast of a sausage-like item, rice and other unidentified foods plus a bottle of water was provided and we were off to the airport for Air Koryo flight JS151 to Beijing. The only other flight on the board was to Vladivostok in Russia. We said goodbye to our three guides, who were exactly that, as opposed to heavy security, and at Gate 3 was Tupolev Tu-204 P-633. It was only partly full, and the whole of the back was empty. We were due to pushback at 8.30am and were, in fact, wheels up at 8.31am for the just under two-hour sector to Beijing. We were offered a cold burger-like item on a bun and a soft drink. The Chinese capital was to be our home for the next couple of days before Finnair took us to Helsinki and then London, from where we returned home.

Conclusion

The bucket list had been ticked and the word that summed up the whole experience was 'surreal'. The citizens of North Korea had shown us what we wanted to see, and we were able to take far more pictures than we might have expected. When we left, there was no heavy security, and nobody was inspecting our cameras' memory cards. If asked if I would go again my answer would be yes, if there was another airshow with different types to see.

To sum up, we had seen far more aircraft than we would have dared to hope and we saw them close up with no restrictions on pictures. When in the park, we saw ordinary people doing the things in a park that people do all over the world. At no time did the people we saw show us any ill will; and the sun shone almost every day. The one thing I have learned during my travels around the world is that the ordinary people are generally nice and want to have a normal, happy life, an aim not always shared by their governments in far too many cases, with North Korea being one.